INDEX

4   **TOWARDS ANOTHER WORLD OF GIG WORK**
Mark Graham and Joe Shaw | *University of Oxford*

7   **WE DON'T HATE THE GIG ECONOMY, BUT IT MUST CHANGE**
Guy McClenahan | *Deliveroo Courier*

10   **THE PEOPLE'S DISRUPTION**
Trebor Scholz | *The New School*

13   **GIVING UBER DRIVERS A VOICE IN THE GIG ECONOMY**
Dawn Gearhart | *Teamsters Local 117*

16   **FIFTEEN CRITERIA FOR A FAIRER GIG ECONOMY**
M. Six Silberman | *IG Metall*

20   **WE ARE NOT ENTREPRENEURS**
Mags Dewhurst | *Cycle Courier*

24   **TOWARDS INCLUSIVE, EMPOWERING DIGITAL LABOUR MARKETS**
Christina Colclough and Philip Jennings | *UNI Global Union*

26   **THE RIGHT TO REFUSE WORK**
Nick Srnicek | *King's College London*

28   **YOUR ROLE IN CREATING A FAIRER WORLD OF WORK**
Mark Graham | *University of Oxford*

32   **REGULATING FOR A FAIRER WORLD OF WORK**
Janine Berg | *ILO* and Valerio De Stefano | *BOFZAP*

TOWARDS ANOTHER WORLD OF GIG WORK

Mark Graham and Joe Shaw
Alan Turing Institute
University of Oxford
mark.graham@oii.ox.ac.uk | joe.shaw@oii.ox.ac.uk

People around the world are waking up to a new world of work. A system that distributes millions of jobs, but no stable work. A system that connects bosses and workers who sometimes never meet each other. A system that offers workers freedoms, but no security or control.

The 'gig economy' is disrupting industries, professions, and livelihoods. But what is actually new about it? Despite mass automation, billions of dollars of private investment, and millions of smartphone apps, work is still work. The old idea of one person paying another to do something for them is yet to be superseded by any great invention. It's just that in some cases the tools of the trade have gone digital, and are likely to remain so.

Despite this reality, a range of new platforms have boldly claimed to revolutionize the old and troubled relations between employers and workers. Uber have disrupted the (often maligned) taxi firms of old; TaskRabbit offers very real and affordable helping hands around the world at the touch of a screen; and Deliveroo has assembled a new army of cycle couriers, ready to pedal through the cold and rain with your evening takeaway meal.

If you read the marketing material of these companies, it sometimes seems like the awkward politics of labour exploitation have been cleverly solved; or that they can be engineered away. But have such old troubles really vanished? Are the old politics of unions, collective bargaining, and exploitation really going to disappear with the download of these new digital platforms?

This small collection of articles from people working within, around, and for the gig economy says no. These problems are far from being solved. Rather, the gig economy has both created new labour markets and transformed (some) old ones. And, with these changes, the old challenges and politics of work have not disappeared, they've just taken on new shapes and forms.

If you get work from Uber, Deliveroo, TaskRabbit or any other such organization, you're likely to know all this already. But for the rest of us, these changes might be invisible. We might not know that our takeaway dinner was going to be delivered by an underpaid, over-worked bicycle courier; we might not have realised that our office party drinks were catered by part-timers using an app; and we might not realise that the reviews we read online are often the product of enormous distributed 'click farms' of ultra low-paid, highly casual-

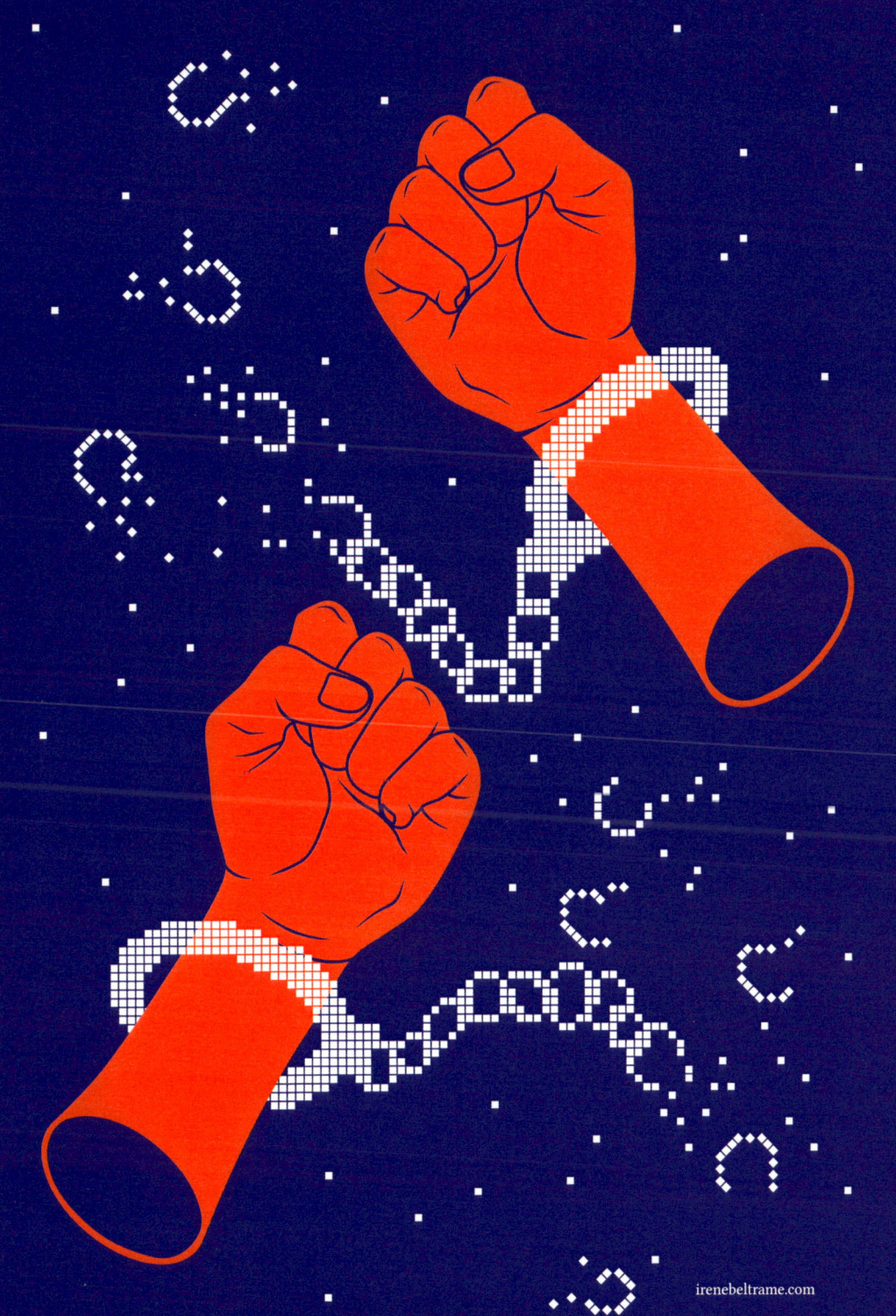

ized labour who have never been to the places or bought the products they are reviewing. A click that you make, or a tap in an app, can set into motion any one of these chains of events.

The collection of articles in this pamphlet sheds light on some of these new practices of work. Whilst exploitation is nothing new, we see innovative ways in which it is being put into practice with the aid of digital technologies: through bypassing legal regulations that afford worker rights to breaks, minimum wages, or proper disciplinary protocol; by ensuring the workers bear the risks of en-

another. While the gig economy offers jobs and income to many in need, it also represents a system with the capacity to exploit and alienate workers in new and innovative ways.

Yet, it doesn't need to be this way. This pamphlet seeks not just to describe this new world of work, but also to change it. It asks what is new about gig work; what isn't; and, most importantly, what we can—and should—do about it. The articles in the following pages showcase some of the battles and struggles faced by gig economy workers, point to ways that the gig economy might be better regulated,

...the gig economy has both created new labour markets and transformed (some) old ones. And, with these changes, the old challenges and politics of work have not disappeared, they've just taken on new shapes and forms.

trepreneurs, but rarely actually have any control over the means of production and distribution; by profitably and opaquely re-writing algorithms that program the daily work of an individual thousands of miles from their employer; by creating global markets with an enormous oversupply of labour power, thus weakening the bargaining power of workers; or by distributing workers in ways that inhibit their ability to communicate with one

and showcase initiatives and strategies that workers themselves might adopt. The history of work will be shaped not just by digital tools and technologies; not just by Silicon Valley capitalists and CEOs; it will also be shaped by the desires and hopes of workers around the world—who, by finding ways to cooperate—could bring a fairer world of work into being.

WE DON'T HATE THE GIG ECONOMY, BUT IT MUST CHANGE

Guy McClenahan, *Deliveroo Courier*
Vice-Chair of the Couriers & Logistics Branch
Independent Workers Union of Great Britain (IWGB)
hi@guymac.eu

Weaving through traffic. Battling pouring rain. Dodging drivers turning across you. It's great to have a job carving through the streets with no manager, but it is a dangerous one. As a courier, you're public enemy number one—hated by pedestrians, motorists and taxi drivers alike. Not that I don't enjoy it—it's great to sit back, coming down a hill with the lights of the city spread out in front of you, the roads quiet late at night. Most people would say that riding is their job satisfaction—people don't just do it for the pay. It's for the sense of freedom that you only get as a messenger; nobody knows the city quite like us. Roaming through the backstreets to kitchen doors, and crossing estates so quietly you surprise the foxes, you get to see a side of your city that nobody else does.

I started with Deliveroo back in October 2016—they were so desperate for riders there was little barrier to joining. Everyone I was with passed the initial assessment (some surprisingly so), and a week later, after handing over your £150 deposit, you had your box and jacket. The first couple of weeks were pretty tough, thrown in at the deep end in Brighton's rush hour with Key Performance Indicators to meet and money to make. Initially, the money was great—the most money I've ever earned. With most young people bouncing around minimum wage jobs, I was doing four or five deliveries an hour, at £4 a pop. (My thighs suffered for this every Monday morning.) With a shortage of riders, there was as much work as you could do—but nobody particularly rushed. "If I can do four drops this hour, and keep up that pace, why tire myself out?", people would say as they rested at the zone centre (where the app sends us to wait).

Over the next few months, as the amount of riders in Brighton reached saturation, things began to deteriorate. People realised that such a lucrative deal was never to continue—but when it starts to drop below a real living wage of £8.45, it begins to hurt. Riders saw that drops weren't shared out fairly. Sometimes there would be 20 of us, sat in the cold on a bench, ready to leap into action at the company's whim—but they'd call in someone from across town to pick up multiple orders at once from the very restaurant we were sat outside. Wages plunged and kept going—and there were nights when people would be out all evening, after Deliveroo emailing us to warn us of Extremely High Demand!, to

only complete a couple of drops. £8 for a whole evening's dangerous, hard work. It got to the point where, as a cyclist, you only had a couple of hours in which to make as much money as you can. On your marks at 7pm, and ride like a maniac for two hours until they take the work away again—it's a dangerous game.

In February the riders voted to unionise with the Independent Workers Union. As we were planning the campaign, anger among riders boiled over and a wildcat strike was called on a Saturday evening, costing the company thousands of pounds. We had our momentum—but as their company lackey, sent down to shut us up, told us, we are "not entitled to union representation." Well, Deliveroo, that's a whole pile of shit. No worker should be denied the representation of a union—indeed, no worker's contract should threaten them with termination if the worker takes the employer to a tribunal, as ours does. We held protests with air horns, smoke grenades, sound-systems and crowds of angry riders, furious at the exploitation that was occurring on the streets. When you're paid so little, your situation is so precarious that you are utterly dependent on your employer to give you the money you need to live month to month. This needs to change.

Many of the big-name restaurants in Brighton supported our campaign—Burger King, Bella Italia, YO! Sushi; not to mention our MP, Caroline Lucas, and the Shadow Chancellor, John McDonnell. (Not much word from the Conservative party—but then again to be expected as we don't fall into the top tax bracket.) So, it's not surprising that in May 2017, we're beginning to see change. Wages are on the up and jobs are being shared out more fairly. We still need a rise in the drop rate—only a £5 drop allows us to earn better than £8.45 an hour on two drops, once costs are factored in. And our contracts still claim we're self-employed. I've always wanted to be an entrepreneur but I never thought I'd be running Guy's Food Delivery, Inc., even though anyone can see that we are clearly not contractors. The workers at the bottom of the tree shouldn't be bearing all the business risk that Deliveroo takes; a quiet night for orders should mean Deliveroo take a hit, not the poorest in the chain.

We don't hate Deliveroo—we may resent them for how they've treated us, but overall, we want them to succeed—it benefits us as much as it does them. We'd like to form a good relationship with our employer, to the benefit of wages and profits across the board. The practices of refusing to recognise our union and refusing to negotiate are vile and morally repugnant, and this needs to change before we can move forward. The writing is on the wall for Deliveroo; they may not care about us, but we can force them to listen.

More on IWGB Couriers & Logistics Branch:
iwgbclb.wordpress.com | @iwgb_clb | fb.me/couriersandlogisticsbranch

THE PEOPLE'S DISRUPTION

Trebor Scholz, *Associate Professor of Culture and Media*
The New School, New York City
scholzt@newschool.edu

The Internet is slipping out of ordinary users' control. Internet technologies are transforming our workplaces, relationships, and societies, and companies like Uber, Amazon, and Facebook are capturing vital sectors of the economy like transportation, as well as phenomena like search and social networking. But all of us who rely on the Internet have virtually no control over the platforms that affect and inform us on a daily basis.

The power held by these principal platforms has allowed them to reorganize life and work to their benefit and that of their shareholders. "Free" services often come at the cost of our valuable personal information, with little recourse for users who value their privacy.

The paid work that people execute on digital platforms like Uber or Freelancer allows the owners of these platforms to challenge the hard-won gains of last century's labour struggles. Workers are reclassified as 'independent contractors' and thus denied rights such as minimum wage protections, unemployment benefits, and collective bargaining. Platform executives argue that they are merely technology (not labour) companies; that they are intermediaries who have no responsibility for the workers who use their sites. The deep pockets of the venture capitalists behind 'sharing economy' apps allow them to lobby governments around the world to make room for their 'innovative' practices, despite well-substantiated evidence of their adverse effects on workers, users, and communities. At the same time, in the gaps and hollows of the digital economy, a new model is emerging that follows a significantly different ethical and financial logic.

Platform cooperativism is a growing movement that aims to build a fairer future of work. By organizing businesses that value democratic governance and the co-ownership of digital platforms, a broad range of freelancers and co-op members have created a concrete, near-future alternative to the extractive 'sharing economy'. Whilst avoiding techno-solutionism, these new platform cooperatives are poised to reclaim principles like innovation and solidarity by bringing together the rich heritage of cooperativism with the newest Internet technologies.

At least 150 platform co-ops and initiatives supporting them have developed rapidly over the past two years, challenging the practices of the 'sharing economy' and the often misogynist culture of Silicon Valley.

The cooperative platform ecosystem ranges from alternative funding tools, labour brokerages for nurses, massage therapists, and cleaners, to cooperative-

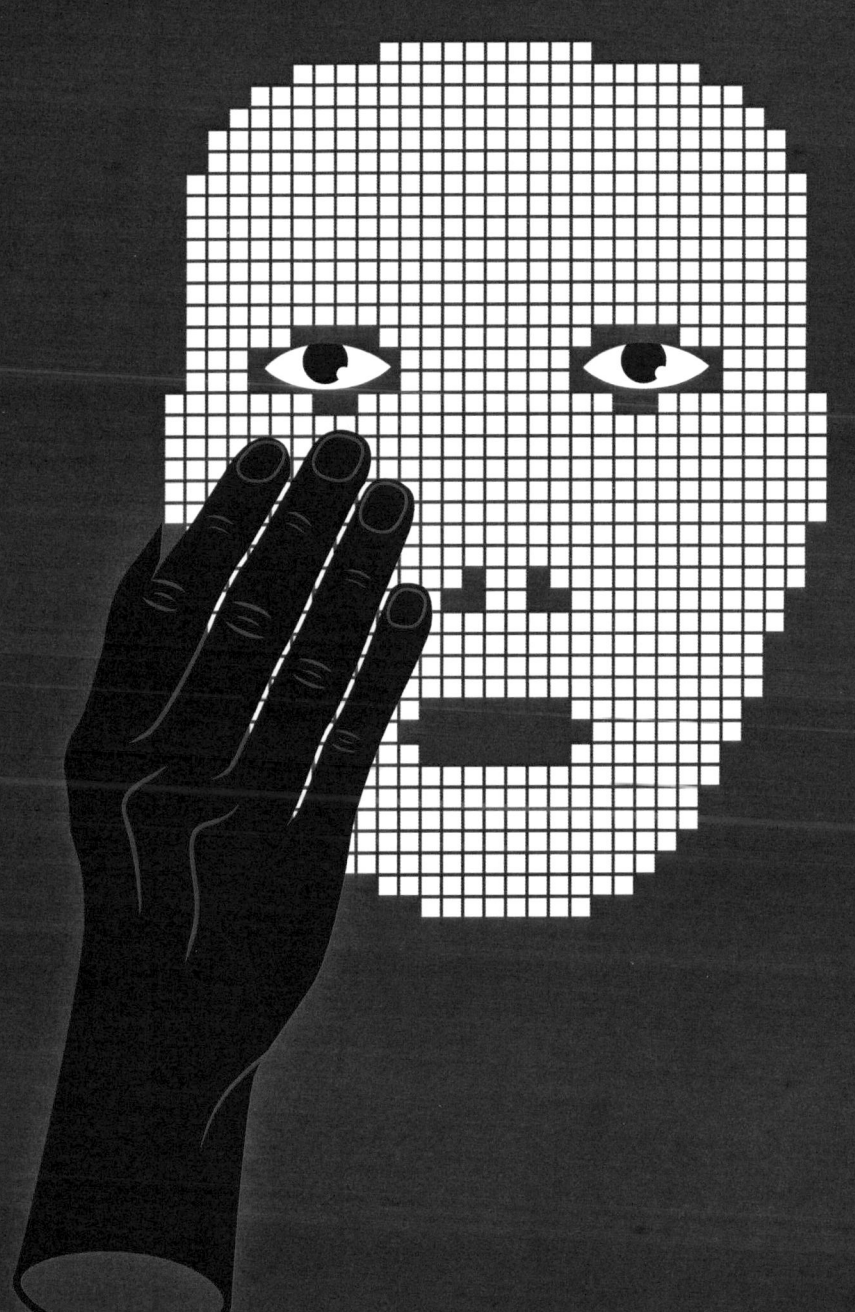

ly owned online marketplaces and data-protection platforms for patients.

Rather than simply posing as a short-term solution for the quick defeat of the extractive investor-owned model, successful platform co-ops have already made—and continue to make—a meaningful difference in the lives of those who participate in them. They are projects that people can work on over their lifetimes. Uber drivers are organizing in co-ops, and designing their own taxi apps. Photographers are offering their work for fair prices on a platform where they're in charge, and journalists are crowdfunding news portals co-owned by their readers. New decentralized networks are enabling people to share their data with each other without relying on a corporate cloud.

Here are some examples. In the United States, Up & Go offers professional home services like house cleaning (and soon childcare and dog walking) to those who are looking for assistance, with labourers from local worker-owned cooperatives. Unlike extractive home-services platforms which can take up to 30% of a worker's income, Up & Go charges only the 5% it needs to maintain the platform.

Similarly, the 25% fee that corporate ride-hail (taxi) platforms extract from drivers has led some drivers to create cooperative platforms across Europe and the United States. Cotabo (Bologna, Italy), ATX Coop Taxi (Austin, TX), Green Taxi Cooperative (Denver, CO), The People's Ride (Grand Rapids, MI), and Yellow Cab Cooperative (San Francisco, CA), among others, have each provided their worker-owners the dignity of a living wage by developing their own taxi apps.

MiData, a Swiss 'health data cooperative', has created a data-exchange that will securely host member-users' medical records. By integrating this traditional health data with emerging data streams from FitBit devices and personal genomic services, MiData aims to out-compete private, for-profit data-brokers and ultimately return the control and monetization of personal data to those who generate it.

As some open-source projects find it hard to pay a dedicated development team, the funding platform Gratipay provides a free subscription-based patronage infrastructure for developers of such ventures. Gratipay provides credit card transactions at cost, subtracting only the processing fees from users' subscriptions. Tools like Gratipay are at the core of the platform cooperativism ecosystem; they expedite the work of other projects.

The Internet can be owned and governed differently. The experiments now underway show that a global ecosystem of cooperatives and unions, along with pro-commons and open source movements, can stand against the concentration of wealth and the insecurity of workers that is the legacy of Silicon Valley's winner-take-all economy. The 'sharing economy' is far more vulnerable than it appears. But building the cooperative platform economy requires innovative organizations, policy work, incubators, experiments, events, research, and community-building work at the grassroots level. Get involved to strengthen our network and shape our work!

Learn more at http://platform.coop

GIVING UBER DRIVERS A VOICE IN THE GIG ECONOMY

Dawn Gearhart, *Policy Coordinator*
Teamsters Local 117, Seattle
dawn.gearhart@Teamsters117.org

Workers are contesting the impacts of centralized automated systems that direct their work.

Since their inception, new companies in the gig economy have touted themselves as organizations that offer opportunities for workers to enjoy the flexibility of being their own boss. Despite the promise of a new type of work, the issues have arguably outweighed the benefits so far. In the shift from human to computer, management becomes automated, algorithms become employers, information asymmetries grow, and preexisting power imbalances are exacerbated. This imbalance is intentionally programmed into the architecture of the platform itself.

In April of 2013, less than six months after Uber's Seattle launch, labour unions in the area received a letter from a driver who wondered what his rights were as a platform worker. This presented an opportunity for the Teamsters union to pivot and innovate in an effort to help drivers make a living wage. The driver and a few of his peers explained that the company often made sweeping changes to working conditions with little or no notice. Those changes ranged from decreases in the per mile fare, to new vehicle requirements. Seemingly arbitrary firings were common practice, as were abrupt changes to the contractual agreement signed by drivers as a condition of using the application.

Unions cannot collectively bargain with an algorithm, they can't appeal to a platform, and they can't negotiate with an equation. The amount drivers might earn is limited, not by a mutually negotiated rate of pay, or by a driver's willingness

Unions cannot collectively bargain with an algorithm, they can't appeal to a platform, and they can't negotiate with an equation.

to work long hours. Instead, worker incomes are limited by real-time adjustments to the rates passengers pay. Earning a living suddenly looks more like a videogame than a job: only with more tangible consequences.

As technology reshapes the way we work, drivers in Seattle have been successfully adapting. The creation of a worker-run organization supported by a traditional union allowed drivers to quickly adapt to the changing power structures at work. The agile design of the App-Based Driver's Association (ABDA) and the Western Washington Taxicab Operator's Association offered a simpler, more direct route to worker voice.

In 2014, a driver named Takele Gobena attended an organizing meeting hosted by Teamsters Local 117 and ABDA. Before working for Uber, Takele was working at SeaTac Airport making $9.45 per hour. At the same time, Uber was aggressively advertising wages up to $35 per hour for drivers. Takele quit his job at the airport, invested in a vehicle, and began working as an Uber driver. After one year on the job, a tax preparation expert informed Takele that after expenses, he made only $2.45 per hour for 2014.

Per-mile rates were slashed by 42% between July and December 2014 ($2.35 down to $1.35). Uber announced rates would be further reduced to just $1.10 by February of 2015. In Seattle, drivers immediately began meeting to develop a strategy to stop the drastic loss of income that would inevitably follow. Drivers mobilized online petitions and joined in mass rallies. Within a few days Seattle drivers successfully forced a reversal of rate cuts back to $1.35 per mile.

Perhaps the most significant driver action to date was the passage of legislation in Seattle to empower drivers in the gig economy. Workers, together with elected officials and community partners, crafted a first-of-its-kind ordinance that officially allowed the creation of unions for gig workers. The law, passed unanimously by the Seattle City Council in December 2015, also compels companies to negotiate with platform drivers over wages, working conditions, and other important issues. New companies like Lyft and Uber, as well as more traditional taxi companies, face penalties for refusing to recognize the humanity and collective voice of workers in the industry.

The legislative intervention model may serve as a new hybrid paradigm for worker representation in an emerging economy. Drivers in Seattle engaged in a traditional campaign to reach the people behind the screens at tech companies. We've learned that worker-directed, community-supported movements can lead to real change. Innovation does not necessitate low wages and a lack of power in the workplace. Instead, emboldening the workers behind the exponential growth of platform companies may pave the way for a just transition to a new world of work.

More on Teamsters Local 117 Union:
http://teamsters117.org

FIFTEEN CRITERIA FOR A FAIRER GIG ECONOMY

M. Six Silberman
IG Metall (German Metalworkers' Union)
michael.silberman@igmetall.de

I have been involved in the 'gig economy' since 2008, when Lilly Irani and I built Turkopticon, a system used by workers on Amazon Mechanical Turk ('MTurk') to review clients. One of our motivations was MTurk's 'rejection' feature, which lets clients refuse payment for submitted work—even if they keep and use the work. While there are good arguments for letting clients refuse payment, the current situation legalizes—even normalizes—what would, offline, be called 'wage theft'.

Since MTurk's 2005 launch, the number and diversity of labour 'platforms'—Upwork, 99designs, Uber, TaskRabbit, etc.—has exploded. The major advantage these platforms offer workers is easy access to flexible work. But because many serious platform workers must choose between platform work and no work—and because platform operators can close a worker's account at any time, for any reason—workers are often hesitant to criticize features that benefit clients or operators at the worker's expense. While platform operators should be applauded for expanding access to work, the imbalance of power—in favour of platforms and clients over workers—designed into most platforms signals a decline in worker rights and bargaining power relative to 'traditional' work. As declining worker bargaining power is linked to growing economic inequality,[1] and inequality threatens democracy,[2] worker rights in online labour platforms should be of interest for anyone concerned with the present and future of democracy. The criteria below are a small contribution to the international, cross-sectoral effort to develop fairer, more democratic online labour platforms.

These criteria are informed by work at IG Metall, the German Metalworkers' Union, my employer, but this article is not an official position statement. Readers seeking an official position can find our "Frankfurt Paper on Platform-Based Work" at crowdwork-igmetall.de and additional material, including platform ratings, at faircrowd.work.

---

1   See e.g. Florence Jaumotte and Carolina Osorio Buitron, "Inequality and labor market institutions," International Monetary Fund Staff Discussion Note SDN/15/14, 2015.

2   See e.g. Christian Houle, "Inequality and democracy: why inequality harms consolidation but does not affect democratization," World Politics 61(4): 589-622, 2009.

1. **Workers should not be misclassified as self-employed if they are employees in practice.** Most platform workers are required to agree that they are self-employed or 'independent contractors', not employees. But some platforms control when and where workers work, penalize them for declining jobs, and set non-negotiable prices and quality standards. Workers on these platforms may in practice be platform employees. Yet thus far courts have considered only a few such cases. A more proactive, robust system for auditing work practices and enforcing employment classification laws is needed. Some national governments are up to the task, but civil society initiatives are also needed.

2. **Strict rules should govern nonpayment (if it is allowed).** Customers who refuse payment for work should be required to indicate in a legally binding manner that they will not use it, and to explain why it was unusable. Workers should have a right to contest nonpayment; such contestations should be reviewed by a human platform employee. If the review outcome is not acceptable to both customer and worker, a neutral third party, funded by customers, workers, and the platform, can make a final and binding decision.

3. **Task pay terms should be clear.** The time in which the customer agrees to review and pay for work should be stated up front, as should the task-specific conditions under which nonpayment, if permitted, is permitted.

4. **Platforms should review task instructions before publication.** This will reduce the likelihood of unclear instructions leading to unsatisfactory work and nonpayment.

5. **If nonpayment is permitted, rates of payment or nonpayment should not be used to measure worker quality.** It cannot be assumed that customers only refuse payment when work is unusable; customers use imperfect quality control processes and sometimes refuse payment as a cost-reduction strategy. Because nonpayment does not necessarily reflect unsatisfactory work, platforms should not let customers screen workers

As declining worker bargaining power is linked to growing economic inequality, and inequality threatens democracy, worker rights in online labour platforms should be of interest for anyone concerned with the present and future of democracy.

based on customer (non)payment rates. Measures of work and worker quality should be separated from payment to reduce the effect of erroneous or malicious nonpayment on workers' access to work.

6. If nonpayment is permitted, customer nonpayment rates should be made visible to workers choosing tasks.

7. Pay should at the very least comply with minimum wage regulations in the worker's location. Additional desirable pay benchmarks include (1) a local living wage and (2) the median local wage earned by workers performing similar work (a) as freelancers, (b) as employees, and (c) as employees with collective agreements.

8. In the event of technical problems with a task or platform, workers should not pay the cost for lost time or work.

9. Workers should be able to contest nonpayment, work evaluations, and qualification test outcomes. In some cases, contestations may be reviewed by a platform employee; in other cases, platform employees will face conflicts of interest and an external mediator will be appropriate. Platforms should contribute to paying for external mediators, along with civil society partners (e.g., unions) and, where appropriate, governments.

10. Customers and platform operators should respond to worker communications promptly, politely, and substantively. There is however a limit to customers' and operators' ability to field requests from unusually persistent or 'unreasonable' customers or workers. Ideally therefore a transparent process should be devised, in which the appropriate parties agree to respond in a given time to inquiries from a given person on a given topic up to some number of times. If the inquiring party finds the responses inadequate, a neutral third party may make a binding decision.

11. Workers should know who their customers are and the purpose of their work. If secrecy is essential, platform operators should work with the customer to disclose some information (e.g., 'a Swiss bank').

12. Tasks that may be psychologically stressful or damaging (e.g., review of social media content for hate speech, violence, or pornography) should be clearly marked. Workers completing such tasks should have access to counselling or support, paid for by the customer and/or platform.

13. Workers should have a legally binding way to make their needs and desires heard to platform operators, such as union membership, collective bargaining, and, in countries with such structures, works councils and co-determination rights. Even for workers who are truly self-employed, platform operators shape workers' ability to get work and their bargaining power with customers. Most workers are not independent business people negotiating 'eye to eye' with customers and platform operators. The fact that current competition law may in some jurisdictions prohibit self-employed platform workers from organizing and negotiating collective agreements with platform operators is not an argument that platform workers should not be allowed to organize but an argument for revising competition law.

14. Worker account deactivations should be reviewed by a human platform employee. Workers should be given reasons for deactivation and have a right to contest it. First review after a contestation may be by an employee; if this review is also contested, a neutral third party should make a binding decision. Platform operators should not be permitted to (even indirectly) punish workers whose deactivation is overturned on external review.

15. Workers should be able to view and export a complete human- and machine-readable work and reputation history at any time.

Acknowledgements:
Thanks to Vanessa Barth for criterion #3.

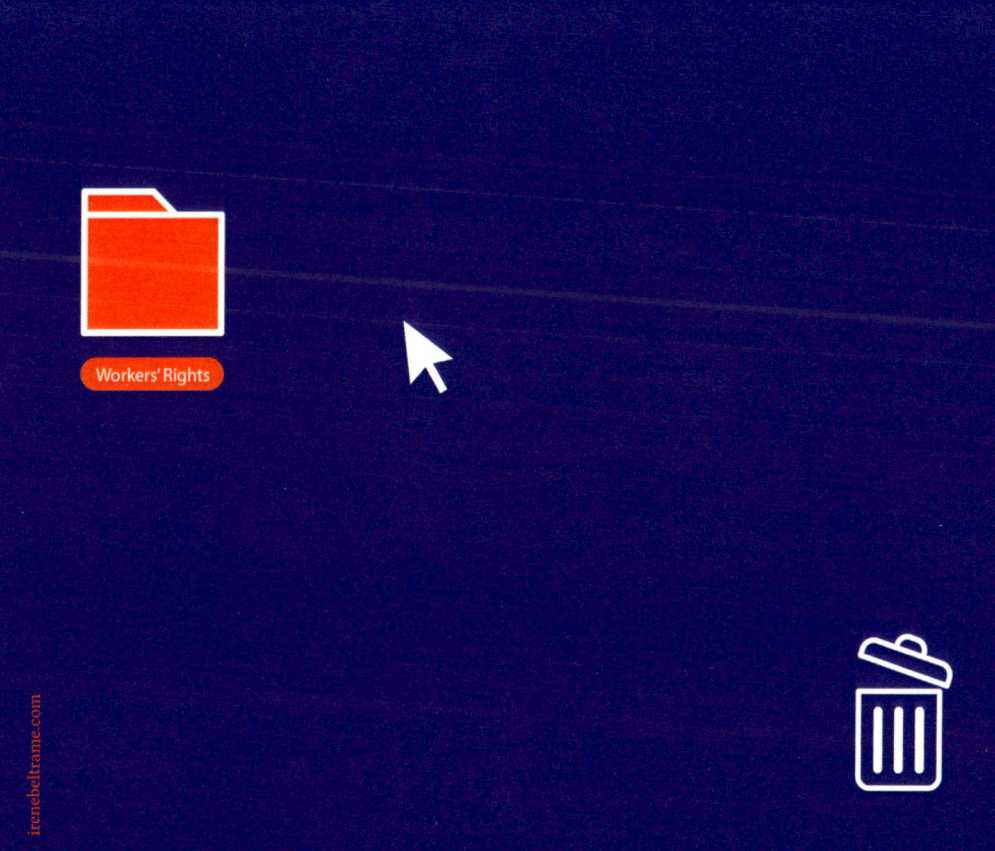

WE ARE NOT ENTREPRENEURS

Mags Dewhurst, *Cycle Courier*
Chair of the Couriers & Logistics Branch
Independent Workers Union of Great Britain (IWGB)
maggiedewhurst@iwgb.co.uk

It's 7.30 pm on a Thursday evening in late March and I get a phone call from an unknown number. It turns out to be a van courier who's read about our union activity online, and wants to know what the union could do for him and his colleagues. He tells me that all of them work in extremely precarious conditions, due to the huge costs imposed on them by the major courier company they work for. "People have to realise they have a lot of power" he says. He's right: they are a multi-million pound business that very profitably employs thousands of couriers.

If you're unfamiliar with the 'gig economy' then here's a brief summary. Corporations set up their business model in such a way that they have a minimum number of formal employees, while 'engaging services' from a large pool of casualized, self-employed people. Even though their staff often can't choose their hours, or realistically take work from multiple employers, these companies refuse to employ staff like the van courier in conventional ways. In other words, people who work in the gig economy tend to be:

• Working on bogus 'independent contractor' contracts, which ensure they have no employment rights of any kind.
• Controlled and/or managed through an app or software.
• Working remotely without a formal workplace, which might be on the roads as a delivery driver, at home as a technical engineer or sales rep, or in multiple workplaces such as a travelling repair person.
• Paid per task, such as paid per delivery or job completed.

The cornerstone of the gig economy is the first point about independent contracting. This fact systematically removes almost every single one of our workers' rights that have been won in the UK. If you've ever had to sign up to one of these contracts, you'll already be familiar with some of the legal clauses that are included to effect this.

For example, the contract is not called a contract of employment. Typically, it's called a 'contract for services', or a 'tender agreement'. This implies that we carry out multiple individual contracts, rather than the reality that we can work for long and continuous periods, and often with just one employer. And although these terms were entirely drafted by one party (the employer), it seems to suggest the terms were negotiated between two commercial enterprises engaging in a trading relationship. Nothing could be further from the truth.

Another term might read: 'the supplier

[that's you] is under no obligation to provide services, and the company is under no obligation to offer services'. This is an even weirder one when you start to work in the gig economy, and you ultimately come to understand that it's a flat-out lie. Of course you're meant to work and they are meant to give you work. That's why you want a job and that's why they're hiring people to provide their product, right? But again, it serves to break down the level of obligation between the parties in order to prevent one party being seen as the employer. If that were the case then they'd have to meet a number of minimum standards, such as ensuring that they pay at least the national minimum wage and a pension. Both of these are undesirable inconveniences for the average gig economy business.

Luckily, clauses like this one have rarely been used against the worker so far, and courts will likely find in your favour—if you can fight it. But clauses like this have been inserted into the contracts of thousands of workers by corporate lawyers in order to attempt to deprive them of basic employment rights. The gig economy is littered with such false contracts—and that's without mentioning the convoluted procedures, arm's length management, automated email disciplinaries or dismissals, and the almost complete transfer of risk onto thousands of individual workers!

All of this might sound totally bonkers, and you'd be right, but the situation is commonplace for the thousands of people who have been forced to become 'entrepreneurs' just to get a job. And in the pro-

> *And so suddenly, because you have the right to subcontract your job, you're no longer entitled to any other rights.*

Finally—and this the big stinger that all the gig economy corporations now want: 'the supplier [that's you] have the right to send anyone on your behalf to perform the services and are responsible for paying that person'. Why? Because it's a way of saying you are no longer a worker, with worker's rights. Instead, you're an entrepreneur, and entrepreneurs take risks (and suffer them too). And so suddenly, because you have the right to subcontract your job, you're no longer entitled to any other rights.

cess giving up any rights as a worker. The result? Modern day exploitation by courier companies that might put you £250 in debt for the privilege of your first week at work—through dispatch fees, rental charges or (often well-hidden) insurance costs. One van driver I know spent £43,000 over three years on van hire through his employer—because he lacked the capital or ability to seek credit elsewhere—and another got hit with unexpected compulsory charges like a £89 windscreen insurance bill. Many others have the price of

a company uniform deducted from their first week's wages—but yet are supposed to be 'independent contractors'!

In none of these situations did the worker really have much option but to hand over the cash—and the company falsely reiterates that this is an 'opportunity' to start a business. Workers around the world are being hit with these conditions, alongside no guaranteed hours, earning less than minimum wage and not getting a pension or paid holiday leave. You might have to deliver 40 takeaways per month just to cover your insurance. Or be forced to work multiple jobs because you can't survive on one without guaranteed hours or pay. I know couriers desperately trying to juggle two or three apps at a time, as they try to feed their kids or pay rent. This situation is unsustainable, un-just and urgent. But what options are left? Carry on being exploited? Wake up in a trap in five years' time? No, we have to fight it now. And we have to fight it because we are workers, not entrepreneurs!

This is what we are doing at the Independent Workers of Great Britain (IWGB) union—and if you work in the gig economy then join us! The process we are undertaking at the Couriers and Logistics Branch is two-fold: we're organizing the workers who work on these bogus contracts, while also engaging in the long and drawn out legal processes needed to challenge and deconstruct these ridiculous clauses. This involves identifying workers with similar problems who share the same employer and trying to achieve the required union representation of 50%. Then we can bargain collectively to try and challenge such exploitation. But this is often very difficult to achieve because the workers are vulnerable, scared and often misinformed of their legal rights by their employer. So first we have to do our best to protect their identity and security, and second we have to help educate them on what can be done—including by helping them bring about a legal case if possible.

It is extremely difficult to unionise in this industry. Yet, what we are doing is a start, and we are welcoming new members every day. We need to do this now because it will take years to fully expose the damage already done by companies such as Uber, Deliveroo, CitySprint, eCourier, Stuart, Jinn, Quiqup and others. This is mainly because people don't yet fully understand how these businesses so thoroughly exploit their workers, but it's also because the workers themselves do not understand what rights they have left. It's not the flexibility and freedom promised by their marketing and legal departments; it's dirty old tricks using fancy new shiny tech. And these tricks mostly revolve around pretending that workers are entrepreneurs. This is what we have to fight for as a union: to educate people in this basic truth and to set out our claims for recognition. We are workers, not entrepreneurs; and this means that we will not stop fighting for our protections, rights, and agency to act collectively.

More on IWGB Couriers & Logistics Branch:
iwgbclb.wordpress.com | @iwgb_clb | fb.me/couriersandlogisticsbranch

TOWARDS INCLUSIVE, EMPOWERING DIGITAL LABOUR MARKETS

Christina Colclough *(Senior Advisor)* and **Philip Jennings** *(General Secretary)*
UNI Global Union
christina.colclough@uniglobalunion.org | philip.jennings@uniglobalunion.org

The gig economy is celebrated by some for its flexibility—enabling workers to earn an income when they want, how often they want, and using existing resources. However, the gig economy is, we claim, one of the key drivers behind an increasing individualization and casualization of work. By claiming that their workers are self-employed, gig economy platforms are in fact abusing human rights. By denying workers of any social rights and social protection, such as the right to sick leave, holiday pay, pension payments, paternity leave and unemployment benefits, the likes of Uber, Deliveroo, Amazon Mechanical Turk, are simply, and crudely put, exploiting people.

Workers on those platforms are fully exposed to the whims of the market. If the demand for their services declines, so does their income. As a result, the worker alone (rather than their employer or the platform) bears a huge amount of risk. The so-called 'flexibility' comes therefore at a very high cost for workers.

Across the world, more and more workers are being pushed into insecure, precarious work forms that deprive them of the right to collectively bargain for decent pay. Competition law in many countries regards the self-employed as companies, and companies have no right to collectively agree on their prices. Put differently—as people are pushed into competition with one another for gig work, they too are pushed out of most, if not all, forms of security and collective representation and action.

This is of course unacceptable! As the rich get richer, the rest are left behind in a growing swamp of exploitation. No politician, no national economy, no morality should accept this. Nor should anyone be seduced to believe that a strong, sustainable and competitive economy has ever, or will ever, be built on extreme inequality. Unfortunately, the rising number of working poor is a sad testimony to the failures of regulators to acknowledge this and stop the exploitation of workers.

UNI Global Union represents more than 20 million workers from over 900 trade unions in the fastest growing sectors in the world—skills and services. A total of 90% of new jobs in Europe are generated in these sectors. We are fully dedicated to turning the tide to make sure that the digital world of work is empowering and inclusive. We are pushing for five key changes:

Firstly, we demand that all workers, in all forms of employment, have the same strong social and fundamental rights. This means that no matter how you are employed, you have the right to leave, to pension, to holidays, to sick pay, etc. You have a right to collective bargaining and the freedom of association. You have the right to human rights, ILO labour standards and the rights that the union movement has fought for, and obtained, over the last generations. All of which seem so foreign to these new business forms. A culture shift in many platforms is needed. It can be done, as our German affiliates so clearly show in their contribution to the crowdsourcing code of conduct. Or our Austrian colleagues have shown by co-creating the first ever work's council in a platform (in Foodora, a bike courier company). Guaranteeing your rights will also require changes to our social security institutions, and will cost money. We therefore demand:

Secondly, that all companies of all kinds, pay their social contributions and taxes due. Flying under the radar, avoiding tax or squirrelling away money in tax havens is unacceptable. Companies, including platforms, rely on healthy, able workers to do their work. All companies should contribute to the societies in which they are embedded and on which they depend.

Thirdly, the digital economy will require that we all engage in continuous up- and reskilling. As robots and artificial intelligence replace and displace workers and work, every worker should have the right and access to training—regardless of their status as employees, contractual workers or self-employed. This also costs money, which is why we demand that all employers, of all kinds, pay into a national education and skills fund that should be governed by employers, trade unions and the state.

Fourthly, we demand of companies that they take responsibility for training, re-training and upskilling current and future staff through extended apprenticeship schemes that are tailored to all types of workers.

Fifthly, the most valuable companies in the world today employ relatively few employees. For example, Apple—the highest valued company in the US—employs 57,000 employees worldwide. In comparison, in 1962, the wealthiest company, AT&T, employed 564,000. The decline in employees is partially due to technology and digitalization, but also that these technologies have created long, complex value chains consisting of many subcontractors, including platforms. UNI demands that the few companies at the very top of the value chain take responsibility throughout their value chains for decent work under decent conditions. Outsourcing to cut costs should not also mean that companies can outsource their responsibility.

Sixthly, the world has moved on and is calling on business to respect human rights, and to introduce due diligence processes to avoid adverse consequences of their behaviour on human rights. It's time for a "Fair Trade" charter or license for platforms in the gig economy.

UNI Global Union and all our affiliates across the world are ready to engage in fruitful, constructive dialogue with gig economy platforms. We certainly have a golden opportunity to shape a sustainable future. We need to speak up, be vocal, and demand action and a change of direction.

Read more about UNI Global Union's opinions and work in relation to the future world of work here:
www.thefutureworldofwork.org

THE RIGHT TO REFUSE WORK

Nick Srnicek, *Lecturer in Digital Economy*
King's College London
nick.srnicek@kcl.ac.uk

With robotics and machine learning advancing rapidly, our labour market looks set to undergo a significant transformation. Economists have warned that up to half of our jobs may disappear in the next two decades, automated away by a new wave of technology. Jobs in retail, logistics, and transportation are likely to take the brunt of the impact, while a growing healthcare sector soaks up some of these newly unemployed workers.

What can we do to prepare for this problem? One common solution that is proposed is more education. An easy political winner (who could be against more education?), it promises to give people the skills they need to get the high-tech 'jobs of the future'. The problem with this proposal, however, is that most jobs of the future won't require vast amounts of education. Forecasts by government agencies, for instance, suggest that most jobs in the future will only require secondary education, rather than any form of higher education. The 'more education' proposal also fails to deal with the lack of jobs. Even if we give people the skills to secure jobs, there still needs to be an economic system that is producing those jobs.

What then can be done? A radical and far-reaching solution is to provide a universal basic income (UBI), whereby the government provides everyone with a basic amount of money to live on. This would be an unconditional and universal grant—there would be no means testing, and everyone would receive it with no questions asked.

The utility of a UBI lies, first, in its ability to give everyone an income even if they can't find a job. As automation and other capitalist pressures reduce the number and quality of jobs, alternative means of reproduction are all the more necessary. A UBI can help in building these alternatives to wage labour. Moreover, a UBI can effectively eliminate poverty by ensuring that people have enough money to pull them above the level of destitution. As it stands today, there are an increasing number of people in poverty and relying on food banks. Many of them are part of the 'working poor': people that are working low-wage, full-time jobs and yet still unable to make enough money to thrive. A UBI can effectively top up their incomes and pull them out of the vicious cycles of hardship and unemployment. The exact amount of a UBI will vary from region to region, but a minimum should be near to the local poverty level—this ensures the ability to survive.

The most important reason to consider a UBI, however, is the radical shift in power that it enacts. Currently, power lies with employers, and not with a large group of workers desperately seeking jobs to make ends meet. The situation is ripe for capitalists to take advantage of workers' desperation, forcing them to work long hours under poor conditions and for low wages. With a UBI, by contrast, workers would have the power to refuse work; to turn down terrible jobs, confident in the knowledge that they'll always have a source of income. Rather than always being subjected to the demands of a boss, workers would have the freedom to choose what to do with their time. A UBI also changes the dynamics of power on a collective level, as workers can find it cy gains popularity, it will become even more necessary to ensure it is a UBI that works for the people, and not one that simply consolidates existing hierarchies of power.

The question that always arises is, of course, how to pay for it. On one level, a UBI can actually save money. Duplicate programmes in the welfare state, for example, could be eliminated (while maintaining targeted benefits). In addition, eliminating poverty can save im-

> *A UBI therefore gives power to workers, and is a means to struggle for even more radical changes. Wage labour continues (and provides incentives for doing socially necessary work like reproductive labour), but it would have lost its coercive force.*

easier to band together—assured of their ability to fall back on a safety net, and able to use it as an indefinite strike fund. A UBI therefore gives power to workers, and is a means to struggle for even more radical changes. Wage labour continues (and provides incentives for doing socially necessary work like reproductive labour), but it would have lost its coercive force. The idea of a UBI is now rapidly gaining traction. We are seeing Kenya, Finland and Canada run tests, while places like India have completed successful trials with a basic income. As the poli-

mense amounts of indirect costs. In the UK, poverty costs around £78 billion annually in public services (e.g. healthcare, policing, housing, etc.)—a sum that could be drastically reduced. Most significantly though, we live in a world where eight men own as much as the bottom half of the world. At the very least, we desperately need higher taxes on wealth and property as an initial measure to solve this problem of extreme inequality. Using this money to fund a UBI would be a simple and effective way to start addressing these issues.

YOUR ROLE IN CREATING A FAIRER WORLD OF WORK

Mark Graham, *Professor of Internet Geography*
University of Oxford
mark.graham@oii.ox.ac.uk

When we use a digital product, service, or even an algorithm, there is usually no way to know whether an exhausted worker is behind it. There is no way to know whether they get laid off if they become sick or pregnant; or whether they are spending twenty hours a week just searching for work, let alone being paid for it. And there is no way to know how precarious their source of income is, or whether they are being paid an unfairly low wage.

What we do know is that digital gig work has global reach and touches a huge number of lives. Today, there are 48 million workers around the world who are registered on online labour platforms, cumulatively doing work that according to the World Bank consists of 5 billion dollars' worth of transactions this year[1].

Gig work offers income and experience to many who desperately need it. But it also comes with ample risks. My own research[2], and the work of others, shows that many workers have jobs characterized by long and irregular hours, intense work, low income, and tedium[3]. The combination of highly commoditized work, and a global market for this work, means that many digital workers feel that people in other parts of the world will undercut them, and take their jobs if they request better working conditions or higher wages.

Digital gig work certainly can, and should, be regulated. However, many countries are reluctant to do just that. Regulators in places like the Philippines or Kenya know that if they attempt to ensure that digital work is properly regulated (by, for instance, enforcing minimum wages), it can flow out of those countries as quickly as it flowed in. Alternatively, digital gig work could theoretically be regulated in the home countries of clients (think, for instance, of German regulators insisting that German firms must ensure certain working conditions are met, no matter where

---

1. Kuek, S. C., et al. (2015), *The global opportunity in online outsourcing*, Washington, DC: World Bank.
2. See geonet.oii.ox.ac.uk for a summary.
3. Graham, M., Hjorth, I., Lehdonvirta, V. 2017. Digital labour and development: impacts of global digital labour platforms and the gig economy on worker livelihoods. *Transfer: European Review of Labour and Research.* https://doi.org/10.1177/1024258916687250.

workers are based). There is, however, little political appetite for such internationally minded regulation, when regulators in the Global North already struggle to protect their own citizens.

Workers themselves also have a role to play in creating a fairer world of work. It's worth remembering that all large work platforms are privately owned: capturing rents by simply connecting clients and workers. As Trebor Scholz points out in this pamphlet, there is no inherent reason why such platforms cannot be run by, and for, workers as so-called 'platform cooperatives'. Co-operatively run platforms would do a much better job of embedding the core interests of workers into their everyday practice. Workers can also attempt to adopt more traditional strategies such as constructing (virtual) picket lines or collectively withdrawing their labour.

However, while such strategies hold an enormous amount of promise, they are also held back by two fundamental limitations in the specific context of gig work that can be done from anywhere (such as that offered on digital labour platforms such as Upwork and Amazon Mechanical Turk). First, the massive oversupply of labour power and the intense competition for jobs on most platforms undermine the potentials of collective bargaining power. Second, the very existence of a huge and global pool of digitally connected workers means that even if good wages are paid to some workers, there is little stopping that work from being re-outsourced. As ever more people from low-income countries come online, expect this large pool of workers (in the context of an under-supply of jobs) to act as a magnet, pulling wages and working conditions downwards.

What else, then, can be done? These are fertile conditions for strategies that demand more transparency in the global supply chains of work. While consumers of products from companies like Starbucks and Cadbury have pressured those companies into ensuring that the entire chains of production are certified as Fairtrade, users of services from companies like Apple or Microsoft have no similar way of persuading those firms to behave ethically. Users of Facebook, Google, and other digital services, sites, apps, and algorithms currently have no idea if the workers that help to create and maintain those services are treated fairly or paid living wages. In many cases, users may be unaware that there are actually any human workers at all behind those services. But the fact that the act of tracing production networks of digital services and products is a challenging task should not deter us from trying.

In much the same way that the Fairtrade Foundation highlights successes and makes lead firms concerned about unethical practices in their supply chains, a 'Fairwork Foundation' could have a similar impact in the realm of digital work. The specific form that such a foundation might take is open to debate (some ideas are outlined in more detail at https://www.oii.ox.ac.uk/publications/fairwork.pdf and at http://fair.work/). But at a minimum, it will monitor and certify chains of digital work: ensuring that key

 *You are enmeshed in complex and invisible networks of work. And with that realization comes the power to collectively make a difference.*

standards such as fair wages and protection against non-payment are met.

A good question to ask at this point would be: 'why am I reading an article about an organization that does not yet exist?' We put this pamphlet together, in part, to stimulate people who might have an interest in changing the current world of work. Hopefully, by now, you might be interested in trying to implement some of the policies and strategies suggested; maybe by organizing as a worker, or by lobbying and voting for those who set the rules. This pamphlet contains a wealth of ideas about what a more just governance of gig work might look like. You might be interested building a cooperative or helping to support an organization that has democratic ownership as one of its core principles. Such organizations are springing up all over the place, and they need your support. But here's something else you can do.

The idea of having more transparent networks of digital work is one whose moment has come. Myself and some core colleagues will welcome all the help we can get in bringing this idea into fruition. But, more broadly, the point of this article is about what you—as a person in the digital age—can do to make a difference. When you go to a shop and buy a pair of shoes or a bar of chocolate, your actions have a tangible impact on factory workers and farmers on the other side of the world. By buying one product and not another—for better or worse—you reinforce the chains that exist in some global production networks, and you undermine others[4]. You support some models of economic governance and deny your support to others. Your clicks therefore tie you to the lives and livelihoods of digital labourers in Manila or Mumbai as much as buying shoes might tie you to a Vietnamese sweatshop or buying chocolate to a Ghanaian farmer.

It is therefore no longer good enough to imagine that there is nothing beyond the screen. Every click you make, every search you perform, and every photo you like reverberates around the world. You are enmeshed in complex and invisible networks of work. And with that realization comes the power to collectively make a difference.

We can demand more. We can insist that everyone that we indirectly interact with in these chains of work is treated fairly and with dignity. Your actions matter; and no matter where you are and what you do, your actions can help to bring a fairer world of work into being.

4 *Ibid*

REGULATING FOR A FAIRER WORLD OF WORK

Janine Berg, *Senior Economist at International Labour Office (ILO)*
and **Valerio De Stefano**, *BOFZAP Professor of Labour Law at University of Leuven*
berg@ilo.org | destefano@ilo.org

The views expressed in this pamphlet are the authors' own and do not necessarily reflect those of the ILO

It is not possible to have fair and equitable societies unless there are laws and policies supporting workers. Getting a good education and improving one's skills will help an individual do better in the labour market. But not everyone can be a banker, lawyer or doctor. Taxi drivers, bike couriers, graphic designers, audio transcribers—all serve important functions that keep cities and businesses running. But for these workers to earn a living wage and benefit from the prosperity of their economies, there need to be policies in place to regulate work.

The platform economy—driven by the Internet and smartphones—has remodelled the everyday jobs of taxi drivers, graphic designers and clerical workers. In the process, these jobs have become more casual, with few workers benefitting from the protections of labour law. Buzzwords like 'favours', 'rides' and 'tasks' have been used to conceal the nature of the work, with the work depicted as being amateurishly carried out as a form of leisure, with no relation to a real job. Alternatively, the work of the platform economy is presented as a new movement of 'micro-entrepreneurs'—who grab their destinies in their hands as they work when and how they want, answering to no-one, and growing their own businesses.

The reality, however, is much different. A survey by the International Labour Office (ILO) of two important microtask platforms found for example that for 40% of respondents, crowdworking was their principal source of income. Workers averaged thirty hours of week on the

> *Buzzwords such as 'favours', 'rides' and 'tasks' have been used to conceal the nature of the work, with the work depicted as being amateurishly carried out as a form of leisure, with no relation to a real job.*

platform and many had crowdworked for several years. Amongst American crowdworkers, 80% earned less than the federal minimum wage.

One of the more troubling characteristics of crowdwork is the burden it puts on workers to continuously search for work. Jobs can be as short as a few kilometres' drive or ten minutes spent tagging photos online. As a result, the 'Turker', the Uber driver, or the graphic artist working on an online design platform must continuously search for work, monitoring their computer screens or smartphones for opportunities. Indeed, in the ILO survey, it was found that workers averaged 18 minutes looking for work for every hour spent working.

Even when jobs span a few hours or a few days, the worker needs to be constantly searching for new work. Ninety percent of workers in the survey reported that they would like to be doing more work than they are currently doing, citing insufficient availability of work and low pay as the reasons they aren't working more. Despite the desire for more hours, many were already working a lot: 40% of respondents reported that they regularly worked seven days a week and 50% indicated that they had worked for more than 10 hours during at least one day in the past month. Low pay coupled with the need to work resulted in workers spending long hours online. And despite being classified as self-employed, workers rarely have the liberty of genuinely self-employed persons. Platforms mediate extensively the transactions they have with their workers, and also between the customers and the workers. Platforms often fix the price of the service as well as define the terms and conditions of the service, or they allow the clients to define the terms (but not the worker). The platform may define the schedule or the details of the work, including instructing workers to wear uniforms, to use specific tools, or to treat customers in a particular way. Many platforms have performance review systems that allow customers to rate the workers, which they in turn use to limit the lower-rated workers from accessing jobs, including by excluding workers from their system. The amount of direction and discipline that clients and platforms impose on workers in many instances amounts to the degree of control that is normally reserved for employers—and that is normally accompanied by labour protections.

Over a century ago, labour laws began to be instituted in various countries around the world. These laws were intended to provide protection to workers in what was recognized as an unequal relationship of exchange between labour and capital, but it also gave authority to managers to organize and direct their employees' work. While the world of work has changed since the first labour regulations were instituted over a hundred years ago, the fundamental reasons for the existence of labour protections—to ensure safe and healthy workplaces, to give workers a voice, and to provide minimum protections with respect to working time and earnings—remain valid.

The protections that labour laws provide are fundamental for stemming the rise in inequality that has beset most industrialized countries over recent decades.

Indeed, an important contributor to inequality in many industrialized countries has been the increase in 'non-standard' employment arrangements, such as subcontracting, fixed-term work, zero-hours contracts and bogus self-employment. With few exceptions, these jobs pay worse and are more insecure. Gig work is simply an addition to the spectrum of casual labour.

With most platforms classifying their workers as independent contractors, the platforms have freed themselves from the responsibilities that employers have in complying with labour rights, including basic protections such as paying the minimum wage, respecting limitations on working hours, providing paid sick leave, making social security contributions, and permitting collective bargaining. And in the process, working conditions and earnings have suffered.

But it doesn't have to be this way. The technology that has allowed the parceling out and distribution of work to the crowd can also be used to regulate that work and provide protection to workers. Technology can monitor when workers are working, when they are searching for work, and when they are taking breaks. For example, Upwork, the online freelance marketplace, offers its clients the option of paying by the hour, as it can monitor the workers by recording their keyboard strokes and mouse clicks and taking random screen shots. Uber expects drivers to have the app on, which can track drivers' whereabouts including their downtime. This same technology can thus also be used to ensure that workers earn at least the minimum wage or, ideally, to regulate the wage agreed collectively by the workers and the platform. If labour protections are put in place, then platforms will have the incentive to re-organize work to limit search time. Technology and better organizational design can help to minimize search time, improving efficiency for all. The technology can also be used to facilitate payment of social security contributions.

Unless governments step in and regulate the platform economy, the 'future of work' will be one of unprotected work and increasing inequality. We have the mechanisms to regulate the gig economy; all we need now is the willpower to do it.